Simply Psalms

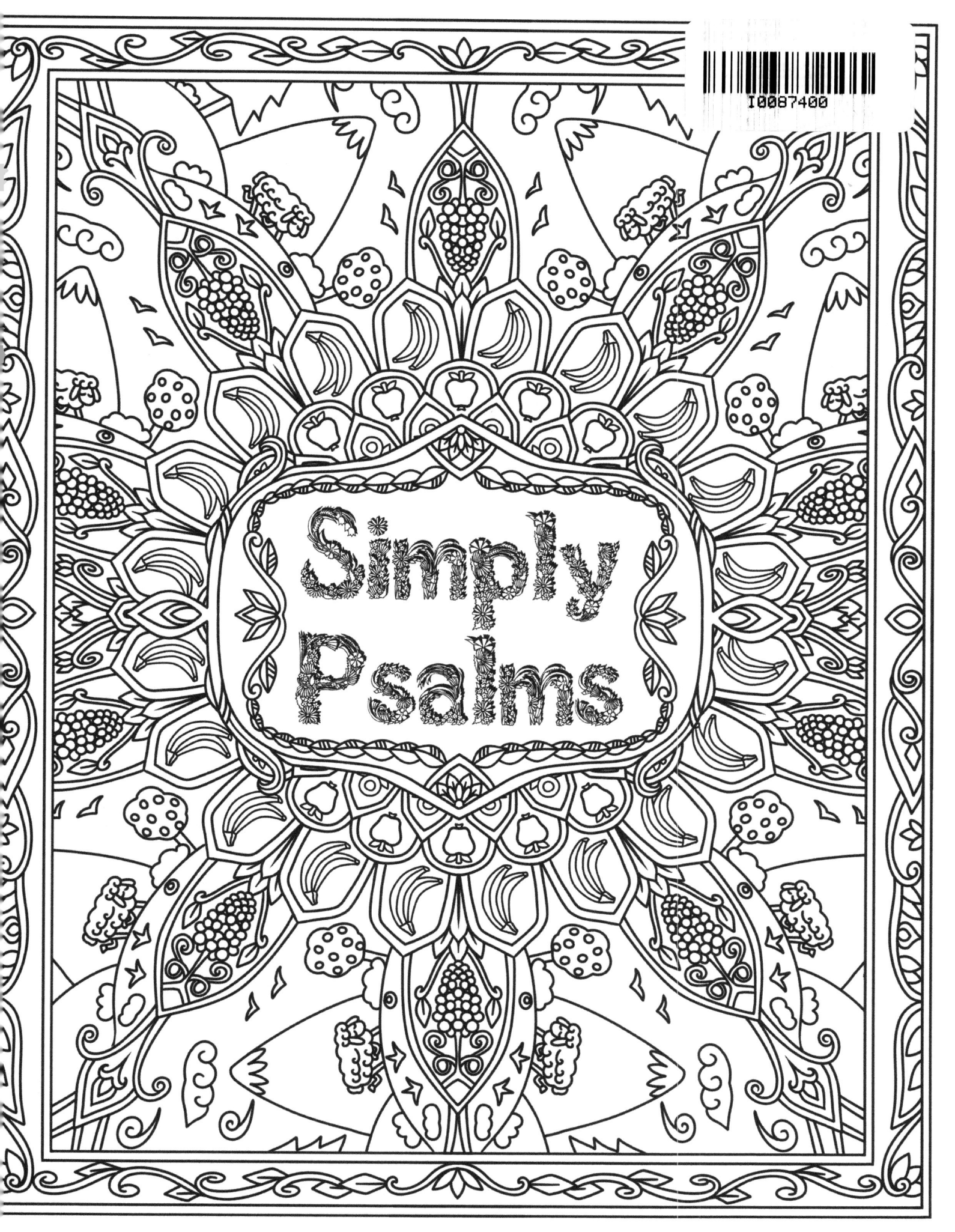

Simply Psalms

edited and designed
by

Keren A. Threlfall

Simply Psalms

Flourish Media
a division of Awesomesauce Publishing

Visit http://awesomesaucepublishing.com/psalm23 for updates and giveaways!

Fonts used in art: Bonjour, Fox and Bear, Faith and Glory, Handsome Hand, Hunterswood, and Have Heart One. (Used with commercial license.)

First edition: December 2015

Printed in the United States of America

featuring artwork and verse texts from:

Psalm 23

Psalm 46

Psalm 121

Welcome to Simply Psalms Coloring Book!

For this coloring book, I have selected three well-loved Psalms from the Bible. There is no commentary or devotional material, only the text. The text on each coloring page is a direct quotation from the particular verse. Because of the familiarity of Psalm 23 in the King James Version (KJV), I have chosen to use this translation for that particular psalm. The text of Psalm 46 and Psalm 121 is taken from the New International Version (NIV) translation.

By slowly working through this book, you may be able to commit each verse and psalm to memory. Using this book for that purpose, you will memorize three psalms.

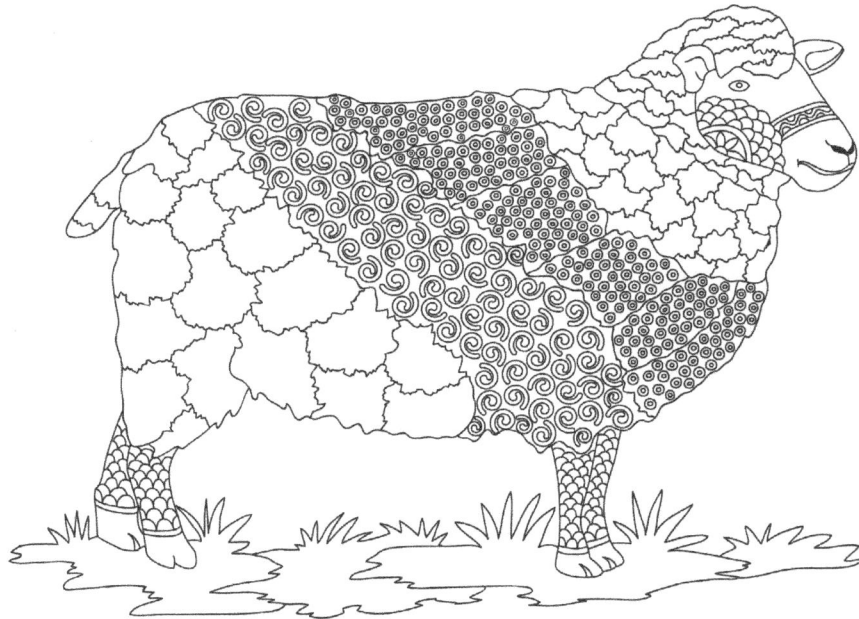

Psalms Selected for This Book

Psalm 23

Psalm 23 is a familiar passage for many Christians. The psalm highlights God's role as Shepherd and King and the way He cares for His flock. If you would like to study this psalm in greater depth, we have produced a Doodle Devotional (devotional + coloring book) dealing only with Psalm 23. (This book is listed in the appendix. Note: The main illustrations for Psalm 23 Doodle Devotional are the same as those featured here.)

Psalm 46

Verse 8 of this Psalm, "God is our refuge and strength, and ever-present help in trouble," has brought comfort to many people in different trials and challenges. The theme of God as our refuge runs heavily through this psalm, with the verses discussing accounts of God's presence and protection. Twice in this set of eleven verses, we are reminded, "The Lord Almighty is with us; the God of Jacob is our fortress." This psalm is both triumphant and comforting, highlighting God's power and exaltation.

Psalm 121

Psalm 121 is one of fifteen psalms (Psalms 120-134), called "A Song of Ascents." The psalm conveys the theme of drawing closer to God. The order, structure, and musical notation of all fifteen Ascent psalms reinforce this theme. This rich and comforting aspect of God's Providence, reminds us that He cares not merely for our body and physical protection, but also provides the care and provision for our souls.

Psalm 23

1

The Lord is my shepherd; I shall not want.

2

He maketh me to lie down in green pastures: He leadeth me beside the still waters.

3

He restoreth my soul: He leadeth me in the paths of righteousness for His name's sake.

4

Yea, though I walk through the valley of the shadow of death, I will fear no evil: for Thou art with me; Thy rod and Thy staff they comfort me.

5

Thou preparest a table before me in the presence of mine enemies: Thou anointest my head with oil; my cup runneth over.

6

Surely goodness and mercy shall follow me all the days of my life: and I will dwell in the house of the Lord for ever.

Psalm 23

Psalm 23:1

1

The Lord is my shepherd; I shall not want.

The Lord
is my Shepherd;
I shall
not want.

Psalm 23: 2

2

He maketh me to lie down in green pastures: He leadeth me beside the still waters.

HE MAKETH
ME TO LIE DOWN
IN GREEN PASTURES:
HE LEADETH ME BESIDE
THE STILL WATERS.

Psalm 23: 3

3

He restoreth my soul: He leadeth me in the paths of righteousness for His name's sake.

he restoreth my soul: he leadeth me in the paths of righteousness for his name's sake.

Psalm 23: 4

4

Yea, though I walk through the valley of the shadow of death, I will fear no evil: for Thou art with me; Thy rod and Thy staff they comfort me.

Yea, though I walk through the valley of the shadow of death, I will fear no evil: for Thou art with me; Thy rod and Thy staff they comfort me.

Psalm 23:5

Thou preparest a table before me in the presence of mine enemies: Thou anointest my head with oil; my cup runneth over.

THOU PREPAREST
A TABLE BEFORE ME
IN THE PRESENCE OF
MINE ENEMIES: THOU
ANOINTEST MY HEAD WITH OIL;
MY CUP RUNNETH OVER.

Psalm 23:6

Surely goodness and mercy shall follow me all the days of my life: and I will dwell in the house of the Lord for ever.

Surely goodness and mercy shall follow me all the days of my life: and I will dwell in the house of the Lord for ever.

Psalm 23

1

The Lord is my shepherd; I shall not want.

2

He maketh me to lie down in green pastures: He leadeth me beside the still waters.

3

He restoreth my soul: He leadeth me in the paths of righteousness for His name's sake.

4

Yea, though I walk through the valley of the shadow of death, I will fear no evil: for Thou art with me; Thy rod and Thy staff they comfort me.

5

Thou preparest a table before me in the presence of mine enemies: Thou anointest my head with oil; my cup runneth over.

6

Surely goodness and mercy shall follow me all the days of my life: and I will dwell in the house of the Lord for ever.

1
God is our refuge and strength, an ever-present help in trouble.

2
Therefore we will not fear, though the earth give way and the mountains fall into the heart of the sea,

3
though its waters roar and foam and the mountains quake with their surging.

4
There is a river whose streams make glad the city of God, the holy place where the Most High dwells.

5
God is within her, she will not fall; God will help her at break of day.

6
Nations are in uproar, kingdoms fall; he lifts his voice, the earth melts.

7
The Lord Almighty is with us; the God of Jacob is our fortress.

8
Come and see what the Lord has done, the desolations he has brought on the earth.

9
He makes wars cease to the ends of the earth.
He breaks the bow and shatters the spear; he burns the shields with fire.

10
He says, "Be still, and know that I am God; I will be exalted among the nations, I will be exalted in the earth."

11
The Lord Almighty is with us; the God of Jacob is our fortress.

PSALM 46

Psalm 46:1

1

God is our refuge and strength,
an ever-present help in trouble.

God is
our refuge and strength,
an ever-present help
in trouble.

Psalm 46:2

2

Therefore we will not fear, though the earth give way and the mountains fall into the heart of the sea,

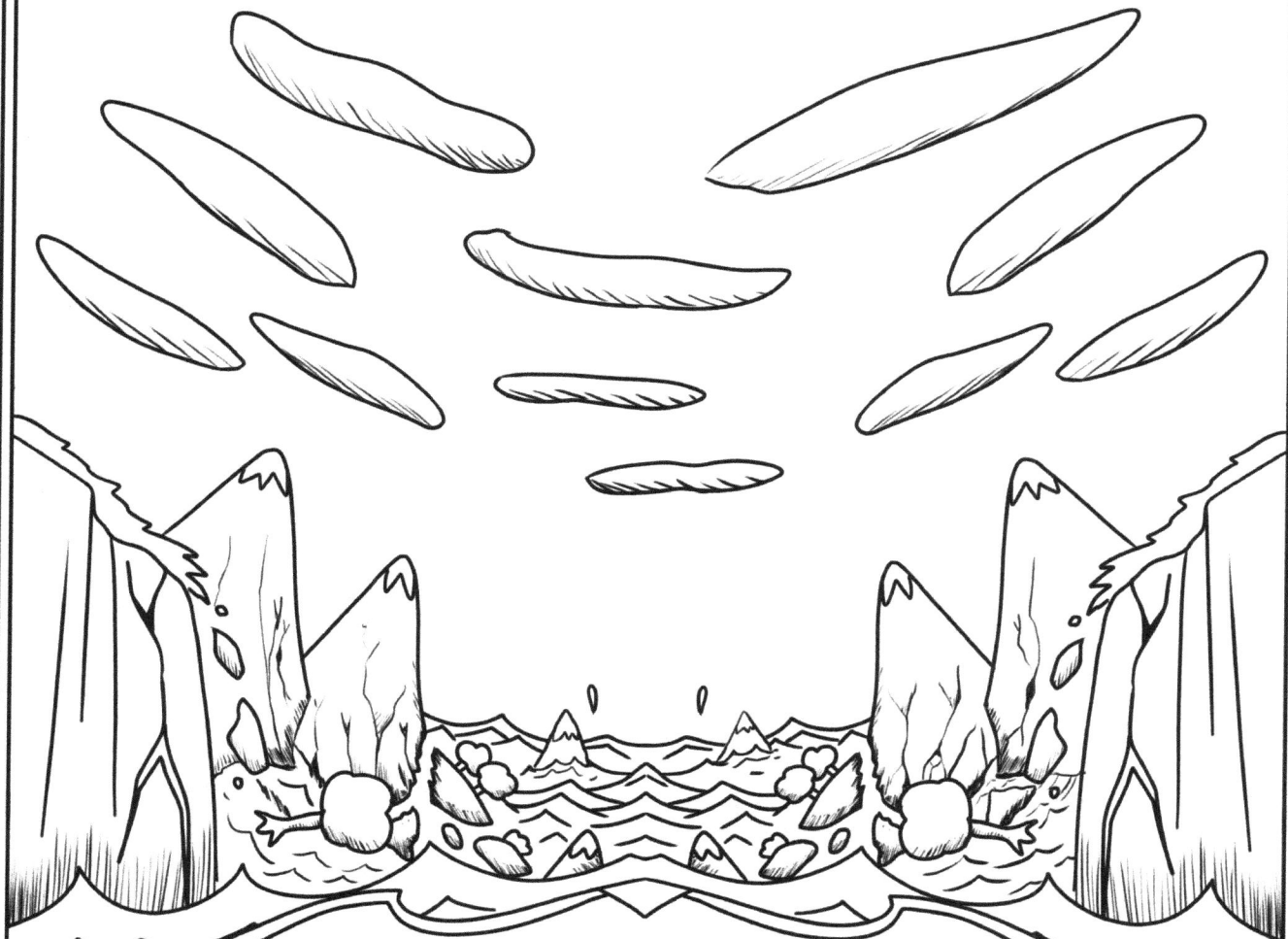

THEREFORE WE WILL NOT FEAR,
THOUGH THE EARTH GIVE WAY
AND THE MOUNTAINS FALL INTO
THE HEART OF THE SEA,

Psalm 46:3

3

though its waters roar and foam
and the mountains quake with their surging.

though its waters roar and foam
and the mountains quake
with their surging.

Psalm 46:4

4

There is a river whose streams make glad the city of God,
the holy place where the Most High dwells.

THERE IS A RIVER WHOSE STREAMS MAKE GLAD THE CITY OF GOD, THE HOLY PLACE WHERE THE MOST HIGH DWELLS.

Psalm 46:5

5

God is within her, she will not fall;
God will help her at break of day.

God is within her, she will not fall.
God will help her at break of day.

Psalm 46:6

6

Nations are in uproar, kingdoms fall;
he lifts his voice, the earth melts.

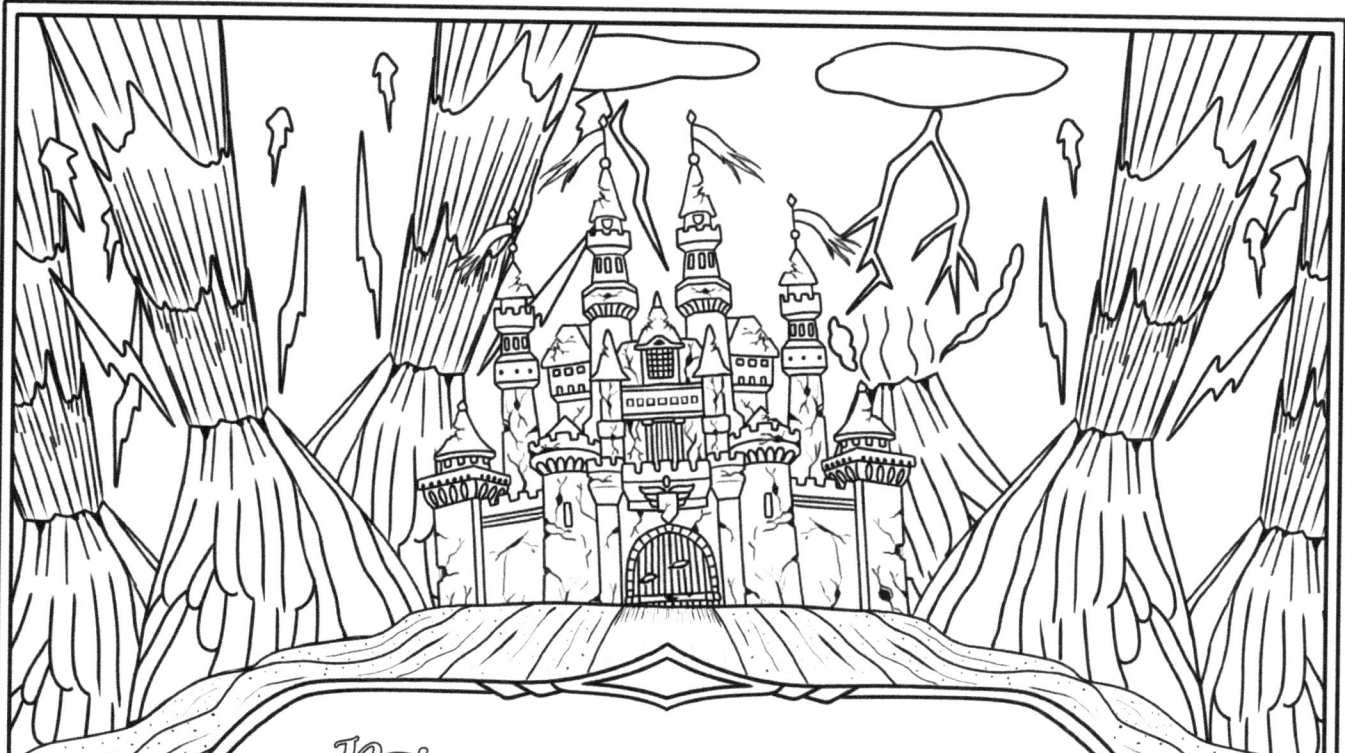

Nations are in uproar, kingdoms fall; he lifts his voice, the earth melts.

Psalm 46:7

7

The Lord Almighty is with us;
the God of Jacob is our fortress.

THE LORD
ALMIGHTY IS WITH US;
THE GOD OF JACOB IS OUR
FORTRESS.

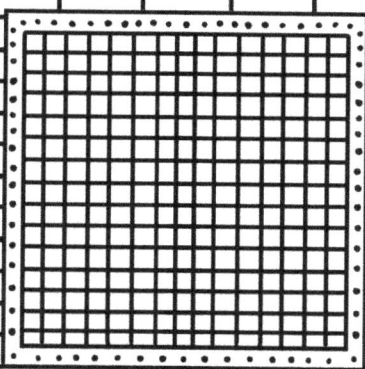

Psalm 46:8

Come and see what the Lord has done,
the desolations he has brought on the earth.

COME AND SEE WHAT THE LORD HAS DONE, THE DESOLATIONS HE HAS BROUGHT ON THE EARTH.

Psalm 46:9

9

He makes wars cease
to the ends of the earth.
He breaks the bow and shatters the spear;
he burns the shields[d] with fire.

HE MAKES WARS CEASE

TO THE ENDS OF THE EARTH.

HE BREAKS THE BOW AND SHATTERS THE SPEAR;

HE BURNS THE SHIELDS WITH FIRE.

Psalm 46:10

10

He says, "Be still, and know that I am God;
I will be exalted among the nations,
I will be exalted in the earth."

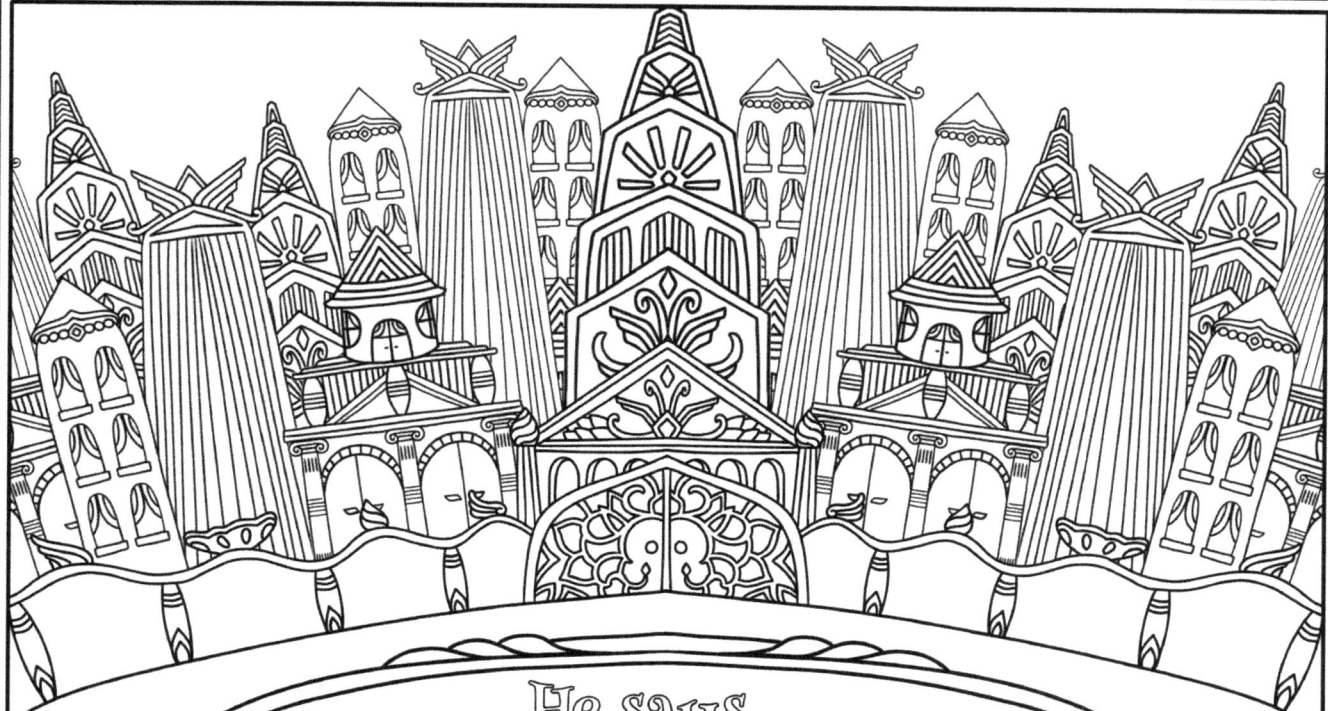

He says,
"Be still, and know that I am God;
I will be exalted among the nations,
I will be exalted in the earth."

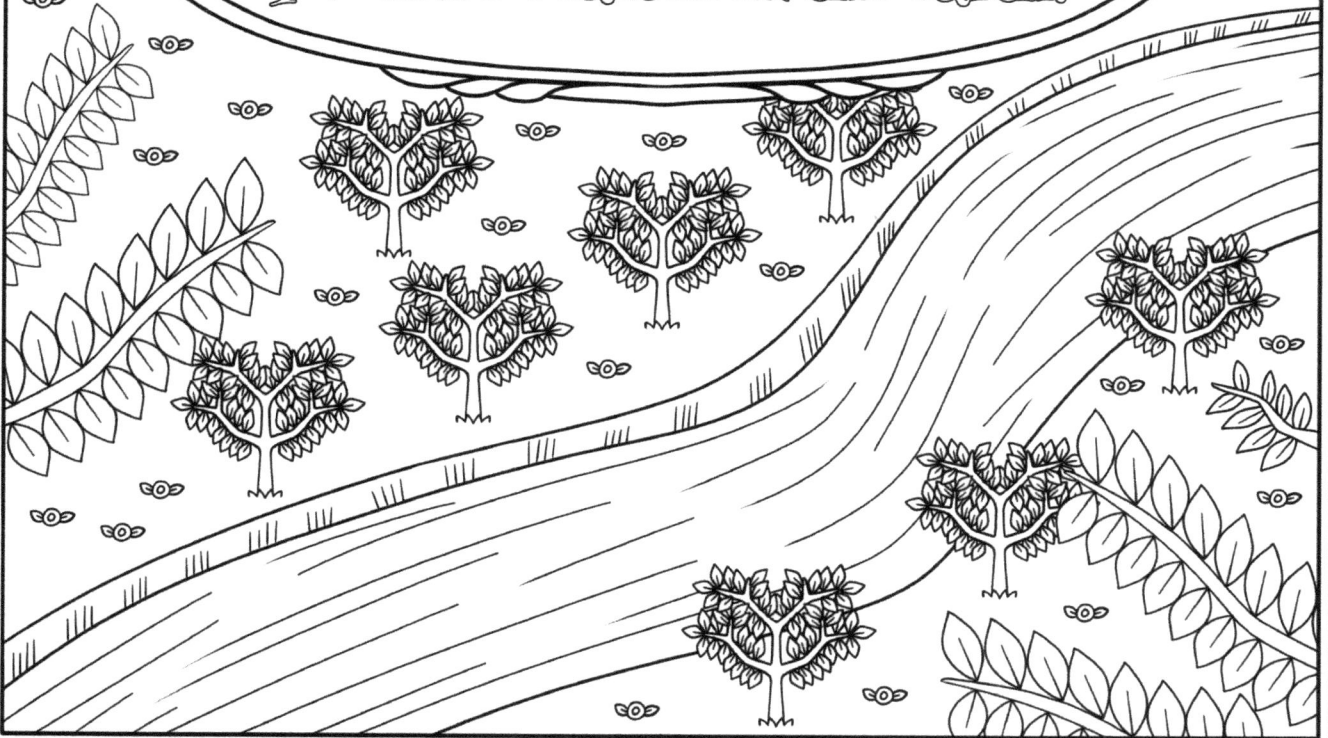

Psalm 46:11

11

The Lord Almighty is with us;
the God of Jacob is our fortress.

THE LORD ALMIGHTY IS WITH US;
THE GOD OF JACOB IS OUR FORTRESS.

Psalm 46

1

God is our refuge and strength, an ever-present help in trouble.

2

Therefore we will not fear, though the earth give way and the mountains fall into the heart of the sea,

3

though its waters roar and foam and the mountains quake with their surging.

4

There is a river whose streams make glad the city of God, the holy place where the Most High dwells.

5

God is within her, she will not fall; God will help her at break of day.

6

Nations are in uproar, kingdoms fall; he lifts his voice, the earth melts.

7

The Lord Almighty is with us; the God of Jacob is our fortress.

8

Come and see what the Lord has done, the desolations he has brought on the earth.

9

He makes wars cease to the ends of the earth.
He breaks the bow and shatters the spear; he burns the shields with fire.

10

He says, "Be still, and know that I am God; I will be exalted among the nations, I will be exalted in the earth."

11

The Lord Almighty is with us; the God of Jacob is our fortress.

Psalm 121

1

I lift up my eyes to the mountains—
where does my help come from?

2

My help comes from the Lord,
the Maker of heaven and earth.

3

He will not let your foot slip—
he who watches over you will not slumber;

4

indeed, he who watches over Israel
will neither slumber nor sleep.

5

The Lord watches over you—
the Lord is your shade at your right hand;

6

the sun will not harm you by day,
nor the moon by night.

7

The Lord will keep you from all harm—
he will watch over your life;

8

the Lord will watch over your coming and going
both now and forevermore.

PSALM 121

Psalm 121:1

1

I lift up my eyes to the mountains—
where does my help come from?

I lift up my eyes to the mountains ~ where does my help come from?

Psalm 121:2

2

My help comes from the Lord,
the Maker of heaven and earth.

my
help comes
from the lord,
the maker of
heaven and
earth.

Psalm 121:3

3

He will not let your foot slip—
he who watches over you will not slumber;

HE WILL NOT
LET YOUR FOOT SLIP—
HE WHO WATCHES OVER
YOU WILL NOT
SLUMBER,

Psalm 121:4

4

indeed, he who watches over Israel
will neither slumber nor sleep.

indeed,
he who watches
over Israel will
neither slumber
nor sleep.

Psalm 121:5

5

The Lord watches over you—
the Lord is your shade at your right hand;

THE LORD
WATCHES OVER YOU—
THE LORD IS YOUR
SHADE AT YOUR RIGHT
HAND,

Psalm 121:6

6

the sun will not harm you by day,
nor the moon by night.

THE SUN WILL NOT HARM YOU BY DAY, NOR THE MOON BY NIGHT.

Psalm 121:7

7

The Lord will keep you from all harm—
he will watch over your life;

The
Lord will
keep you from all
harm— he will
watch over your
life;

Psalm 121:8

8

the Lord will watch over your coming and going
both now and forevermore.

The Lord
will watch over
your coming and
going both now and
forevermore.

Psalm 121

1
*I lift up my eyes to the mountains—
where does my help come from?*

2
*My help comes from the Lord,
the Maker of heaven and earth.*

3
*He will not let your foot slip—
he who watches over you will not slumber;*

4
*indeed, he who watches over Israel
will neither slumber nor sleep.*

5
*The Lord watches over you—
the Lord is your shade at your right hand;*

6
*the sun will not harm you by day,
nor the moon by night.*

7
*The Lord will keep you from all harm—
he will watch over your life;*

8
*the Lord will watch over your coming and going
both now and forevermore.*

Appendix

Resources to Accompany a Study of Psalms

Books

- *Doodle Devotional, Volume 1 - Psalm 23: An Adult Coloring Book Bible Study of Psalm 23* (Keren Threlfall)
- *A Shepherd Looks at Psalm 23* (W. Phillip Keller)
- *Derek Kidner - Psalms 1-72, Psalms 73-150* (Tyndale Old Testament Commentary)
- *Women of the Word: How to Study the Bible with Both Our Hearts and Our Minds* (Jen Wilkin)
- *His Word in My Heart: Memorizing Scripture for a Closer Walk With God* (Janet Pope)
- *The Songs of Jesus: A Year of Daily Devotions in the Psalms* (Timothy Keller and Kathy Keller)

Music

"I Shall Not Want," from the album, *Fortunate Fall*, Audrey Assad

Psalm 23 for Kids, Patricia King & Steve Swanson

Psalms, Sandra McCracken (not specifically Psalm 23)

"Psalm 23 (Surely Goodness, Surely Mercy)," from the album, *Psalms, Vol. 2* Shane & Shane

www.ingramcontent.com/pod-product-compliance
Lightning Source LLC
Chambersburg PA
CBHW0#1228040426

42445CB00016B/1912